IRELAND:
Fifty Pubs in Thirty Days

A Guide to Dublin and Surrounding Areas

Ken Bredemeyer

Photos: Ken Bredemeyer

ISBN: 1496068378
ISBN 13: 9781496068378

Library of Congress Control Number: 2014903925
CreateSpace Independent Publishing Platform,
North Charleston, South Carolina

CONTENTS

Introduction

Day One — Jet Lag Recovery, Dublin 1

Day Two — Getting to Know Dublin 5

Day Three — The Rebellion 9

Day Four — St. Stephens Green 11

Day Five — Getting to Dingle 15

Day Six — The Beauty of Dingle 19

Day Seven — Experiencing Limerick 23

Day Eight — Bunratty Castle and Folk Park 25

Day Nine — Adare Village 29

Day Ten — Back to Dublin 31

Day Eleven — Kilmainham Gaol 33

Day Twelve — Glasnevin Cemetery 37

Day Thirteen — Waterford Day Trip 41

Day Fourteen — A Bit of History 43

Day Fifteen — More History and a Little Shopping .. 49

Day Sixteen — Traditional Irish Music 51

Day Seventeen — The Famine Ship 53

Day Eighteen — Guinness Storehouse 57

Day Nineteen — Shopping North of the Liffey 59

Day Twenty — The North: Belfast 63

Day Twenty-One — Black Taxi Tour 67

Day Twenty-Two — Giant's Causeway 71

Day Twenty-Three   Back to Dublin.................................75
Day Twenty-Four   South of the Grand Canal............77
Day Twenty-Five   Glendalough Day Trip..................79
Day Twenty-Six   Exploring the "Old City"..............85
Day Twenty-Seven   Cong and Athlone.........................89
Day Twenty-Eight   Back to Dublin..............................95
Day Twenty-Nine   DART and the Irish Sea...............97
Day Thirty   Rebel Walking Tour....................101

"The" Fifty Pubs..........................105
Favorites...111
Helpful Web Addresses...............115
Irish Blessing.................................117

INTRODUCTION

Pubs have always been, and remain so today, a big part of Irish life. My wife, Anne, and I, after spending many months in beautiful Ireland over the past sixteen years, have found pubs to be a great source of entertainment, friendship, and information. The word "pub" comes from "public house." In small towns and villages, the pub is an integral part of life, a gathering place for families during the day and early evening and a source of conversation and entertainment as the night goes on.

One night in the small town of Clifden, John, our tour guide and driver for the previous few days, told us that because it was our last night together, he would like to share a pint with us. John had also become a friend, and we jumped at the chance to spend some downtime with him. Later that night, John, with a big grin on his face, said, "You're now breaking the law." He then explained that it was past the legal closing time for pubs, and the doors had been locked. We couldn't tell because the patrons were allowed to stay, they were served, and "the band played on." After an hour or so, John instructed us to stand, as the whole pub did, and the band played the Irish national anthem. Then the night was over. It's just another example of how much the Irish love their country and how patriotic they are.

You'll find that almost without exception, every town and village has at least two churches and a pub. It's said that there are more than a thousand pubs in Dublin alone.

One of the first things you will notice immediately is the cleanliness of the towns and villages. The streets are clean and lined with hanging baskets of vibrantly colored flowers. This is in part because of the National Tidy Town initiative. The Tidy Town competition has created a friendly rivalry among towns to improve the environments in which people live and work. The winning town proudly displays its recognition with plaques, signs, and ads.

You will most likely have to look at a map to remember which towns you visited, given the great number of them that start with *Kil*, *Bally*, or *Dun*. *Kil* means "church," *Bally* means "town" or "place of," and *Dun* means "fortified" or "fort."

There are three things to remember while reading this book:

1. Any negative (or positive, for that matter) comments about any places are my opinion and my opinion alone and should not keep you from seeing for yourself what the places have to offer.

2. When I say to have another pint, it is somewhat tongue in cheek, because you can just as well enjoy a cup of coffee, a cup of tea (except iced tea), or a soft drink. The important thing is to experience the pub culture that is such an intricate part of Ireland.

3. The following is intended only as an example of a thirty-day itinerary and should be altered according to your likes, dislikes, the amount of time you have available, and the weather. Exploring the beautiful country of Ireland and its splendid people is something you will never forget. They say, "You can leave Ireland, but Ireland will never leave you." I don't know who "they" are, but I couldn't agree more!

There is an absolutely lovely lady by the name of Mary O'Grady who can be an enormous help in ensuring that your trip will be a memorable one. I found Mary on the Internet more than ten years ago, and it soon became obvious that she was not only trustworthy but also knowledgeable about travel around Ireland. Mary can set up hotel, guesthouse, and B & B reservations; arrange tours for individuals and groups alike; and give you great advice on what sights to see. Just give Mary an idea of what things interest you, and she will see that you leave Ireland satisfied and longing for your next visit. Mary has set us up with private drivers and group tours, as well as lodging all over the Republic of Ireland and Northern Ireland. For more information, check the Internet at www.irishtravelplans.com or contact Mary directly at maryogrady@eircom.net.

You will most likely find that you often want to make notes on interesting things you have learned about a site you have seen, a term or saying you have heard, or your schedule. For that reason, I have included several blank pages at the end of this book for your use.

Helpful Phrases

"Mind your head": Watch your head, low structure above.

"Mind your step": Watch for obstructions on the ground.

"Dead slow": Drive very slowly, as through a parking lot.

"Traffic calming ahead": Lower speed limit ahead.

"Sorry": Excuse me.

"No problem": Typical answer a waiter or waitress gives when a patron asks for something.

"Bucketing rain": Heavy rain.

"Craic" (pronounced *crack*): Fun, partying, loud, boisterous conversation.

"What's the craic?": What's new? What's going on?

"Our salads have no air miles": Salads ingredients are fresh from the garden, not shipped in.

"Lough" (pronounced *lock*): Lake.

"Collected by": Picked up.

"Publican": Keeper of a public house (pub) or tavern.

"Bit of a head": Hungover (no experience here).

"No overtaking": No passing.

"Bunching traffic": Narrow road.

"Carriage way": Freeway.

"Spot of bother": Angry, upset.

DAY ONE

Jet Lag Recovery, Dublin

Our hotel of choice is the Jurys Inn Christchurch, and if you are fortunate to get room 419, 501, or 507, all the better because these rooms are much larger. It is conveniently located a few minutes' walk to the city center, it is reasonably priced, and the staff is very accommodating (which is the norm for Ireland).

Having arrived in the morning on our last trip and unable to check into our room, we left our luggage with the hotel and headed off, bleary-eyed, to O'Neills, one of our favorite pubs, for a pint and a place to vegetate until our room was ready. We arrived just as they were opening and were immediately offered a seat, a drink, and conversation about our stay in Ireland. A few minutes later, the manager brought over several brochures of sights she thought we might be interested in seeing. This is just one example of the type of hospitality you find in the pubs of Ireland. O'Neills is also a great place for a tasty, reasonably priced meal. Some of the best food is found in pubs, and O'Neills is at the top of that list. O'Neills's "carver" has a big variety of Irish favorites but serves a mean hamburger, too. No matter what you choose, you won't leave hungry.

After a few hours of relaxing, it was back to the hotel for a long nap to prepare for a little sight-seeing, a good meal, and a pint or two.

A good way to get a feel for the area after a little rest is to take the short walk to Grafton Street, the pedestrian "shopping" street, to get some exercise and see the numerous street performers. You'll see musicians, dancers, puppeteers, and a variety of other arts, ranging from very good to—well, let's just say they should get a different "day job." After your exercise, head around the corner to O'Neills for dinner.

This might be a good time to mention that you need to put your thoughts of the building and health codes that you are used to out of your mind and just go with the flow. It is my belief that pub restrooms are cleaned once a day, whether they need it or not. It's not a bad idea to have a small container of hand sanitizer with you. After a great meal and a pint, you might want to call it a night and head back to the hotel. We last visited in July, a time of year when it is daylight until after ten o'clock, so sometimes it's hard to get a feel for how long you've been exploring without a watch. A few doors down from the hotel is a pub called the Bull & Castle, so it is a good place for one last pint before bed. The Bull seems to be popular with the young people, but we were not impressed with the food or atmosphere. You could also cross the street from the Bull to the Lord Edward. The Edward is only one door from the Jurys and is a small, no-frills pub that caters to the locals. I personally loved sitting in the little cubicle for two in the corner and sharing stories of our day's experiences.

DAY TWO

Getting to Know Dublin

The Jurys Inn offers a rate that includes a full Irish breakfast. Irish breakfasts are large and include items I would ordinarily not eat for breakfast, such as pork and beans, black and white pudding (blood sausage), and broiled half tomatoes. They are delicious, but we found that if you are going to be in Ireland any length of time, you quickly tire of the same thing for breakfast every day.

After a late breakfast, I would suggest stopping by the office of tourism across from O'Neills to pick up brochures for some of the many sights of interest in the area. You can also book tours, purchase train and bus tickets, buy gifts and souvenirs, and get general information on any questions you may have. A great way to get the lay of the land is to purchase a day ticket for the Dublin city tour that operates a hop-on, hop-off bus. It's a perfect way to learn of sights you might want to return to and spend more time. We usually use the first full day to make a plan for which sights we want to see and which days we will go to see them. Remember, be flexible because weather can often dictate where and when you can enjoy certain attractions and sights. As we were told many times, if it's not raining, it will be. But remember: you can always find a pub to duck into to stay dry, get a bite to eat, enjoy a pint, and, almost without exception, meet new friends, both local and tourists.

A great place to jump off the bus and spend several hours is Phoenix Park. It is the largest urban park in Europe, consisting of 1,760 acres. Numerous quiet walkways are available that enable you to stroll through the beautiful landscape adorned with lakes, swans, and flower gardens. It was originally established as a royal deer park in the seventeenth century and is still the home to a herd of around five hundred wild fallow deer. The homes of the Irish president and the US ambassador are on the grounds, as is the Dublin Zoo. Leo, the first MGM lion, was born at the Dublin Zoo, although his original name was Cairbre.

Phoenix Park, Dublin

When you have had your fill of tranquility, hop back on the bus and head for your next experience. We usually get off at the office of tourism and take a leisurely walk back to the hotel for our afternoon siesta. Most days we take a break from the walk at a place called Peadar Kearney's at 64 Dame Street, where we stop for a pint. It's on the north side of Dame Street and is roughly halfway between Jurys and the office of tourism. Its bright green exterior makes it easy to find, and the front opens up onto Dame Street, enabling patrons to watch passersby while enjoying a cold one. However, we prefer to sit in the back. This pub quickly became one of our favorites because of the friendly staff. We got to know the bartenders, and after only one time there, they remembered what brand of beer we drank and that Anne liked ice with her beer. This pub caters to both locals and tourists and is a great daytime stop. It, like most pubs, gets crowded at night, and we found the entertainment hit-or-miss as far as quality. One of the bartenders also publishes *Cheers*, a free magazine that features local attractions, restaurants, pubs, and night spots, with a map showing their location. It's a great help with ideas for lunch, dinner, or a pint. It was from this bartender that we learned of our favorite restaurant, Darwins, which I will discuss later.

A couple of things I should note while I think of it. (1) Most places don't offer table service; you need to go to the bar to order, pay, and pick up your items. (2) Ice is not readily used; most of the time, when you ask for ice, you will get only two or three cubes, even with a room-temperature bottle of soft drink.

After a short rest, it's time to head over to the Temple Bar area for dinner. There are numerous places to eat, and we chose the Quay's at 12 Temple Bar, which has a great upstairs restaurant with good food at reasonable prices. There is after-dinner entertainment in both the restaurant and pub below. The pub at the Quay's is a pleasant place to have a pint or two.

Most places offer entertainment, so you can stay where you eat, or you can explore the many different places and types of entertainment. You'll find that entertainment ranges the full gamut, from traditional Irish to country and western. Entertainment usually starts around nine and ends around two in the morning, with some places offering additional late-night hours. It's hard to find a pub that isn't crowded, especially Friday through Monday nights. Most are busy from four to six or seven o'clock, and then they pick up again around entertainment time, unless you happen to be in the country during the World Cup or another major sporting event that is being televised. Then all bets are off, and it's every man or woman for him or herself.

DAY THREE

The Rebellion

One of the most informative and educational activities, a "must" if you are the least bit interested in the history of Ireland, is the 1916 Rebellion Walking Tour. From Monday through Saturday, it starts at eleven thirty from the International Bar on Wicklow Street, which is a nice place to have a quick bit of refreshment before your tour. You can purchase tickets from the guide at the time of the tour. The tour takes about two hours and proceeds at an easy pace. Our guide was Lorcan Collins, who is the coauthor of *The Easter Rising: A Guide to Dublin in 1916*, a good read that can be purchased from the guide at the time of the tour. Lorcan is extremely knowledgeable, interesting, and entertaining. You will hear about the main players in the rebellion and stand at the location where the rebels gathered before dispersing to take up their posts at St. Stephen's Green, the Four Courts, Jacob's Biscuit Factory, and the General Post Office (GPO). You'll learn the importance of these locations and others, who was in command of each post, their successes and failures, what happened to them during and after the rebellion, and why many Irish men and women went from disliking them and what they were doing to supporting them. This eventually led to a free Republic of Ireland.

Lorcan was more than willing to visit with us, answer questions, and sign his book after the tour. Again, this tour is a must. (Another great rebellion tour will be discussed in the Day Thirty section.)

The walking tour ends at the GPO on O'Connell Street, where there are many great places to get a pint and a bite to eat. One of our favorite pubs in this area is the Oval at 78 Abbey Street Middle. It's a great place to have soup and a sandwich and meet some interesting locals. Another comfortable place to get good grub and a pint is Madigan's at 25 North Earl Street. Both of these pubs are just off O'Connell Street. We didn't spend much time on O'Connell because it has more department store shopping than interesting sights.

The rest of the day is best spent strolling around the River Liffey. Most attractions are on the south side, including the Temple Bar area, Dublin Castle, and Trinity College. There are still many treasures to be found, no matter which side of the Liffey you are on. Be adventurous and find someplace for dinner you would not ordinarily try.

DAY FOUR

St. Stephens Green

On the short walk to the city center, you will pass by Dublin Castle, the center of British power in Ireland for more than seven centuries until the new Irish government took over in 1922. Anne and I were invited to a private function at the castle, where we were fortunate enough to meet a past president of Ireland, Mary Robinson, who was also the first female president of Ireland. We were given a private tour of the castle, and I must say, the history is quite impressive. Be sure to take a little time to see it.

Weather permitting, stop and get a sandwich and drink to go at one of the many sandwich shops (O'Briens comes to mind) and spend the day in St. Stephen's Green. Located at the end of Grafton Street and across from the Stephen's Green shopping center, St. Stephen's Green is twenty-two acres of tree-lined paths, lush foliage, beautiful flower gardens, fountains, and a lake. It's a popular place for families to bring the kids to play and feed the ducks and swans. Many businesspeople come to sit on the grass and enjoy their lunches. Park benches are scattered conveniently throughout the park for comfort and people watching. We actually struck up a conversation with a gentleman who had relatives in our small town in Arizona. He was wearing a shirt with the logo of one of our local eating establishments, which just proves it really is a small world.

We heard a unique story about the battle that took place in St. Stephen's Green during the 1916 uprising. It seems that twice a day during the conflict, the groundskeeper would wave a white flag from his quarters, and the battle would stop so he could feed the ducks.

Caretaker House, St. Stephen's Green

For an afternoon break, cross Merrion Street to Dawson Street and you will find a small red door, if you look closely, with a sign that says "Dawson Lounge." It is on the north side of Dawson, two or three doors from the corner. Through that door and down the stairs, you will find Dublin's smallest pub. They say it's a great place if you have too many pints because it's so small you can't fall down. Although I didn't test this theory, the pub *is* small but worth the stop. A number of good restaurants and pubs are located within a few blocks of Dawson Lounge, so explore. I also suggest the Fire Restaurant for dinner, which is also on Dawson Street.

DAY FIVE

Getting to Dingle

Traveling around Ireland by train or bus is simple and affordable. You can purchase what is called an Open Road Pass for the bus at either the office of tourism or the bus station. A variety of options are available, such as three travel days out of six consecutive days, or four out of eight consecutive days. You just need to decide where and when you want to go and how many days of travel, and then you purchase your ticket. Everyone has heard of the Ring of Kerry, which is beautiful, but the town of Dingle and the Dingle Peninsula are every bit as picturesque and much less traveled by tourists. From Dublin, it takes a day by bus to get to Dingle town with one transfer. Pack light because the bus drops you off curbside on the main street and you will have to walk to your hotel. We found the Dingle Bay Hotel a great place to stay. It is only a few blocks from the bus stop, overlooks the bay, and has both a restaurant and pub. Plan to spend at least two nights because you will arrive late afternoon the first day and won't have the opportunity to enjoy a lot of the sights that day. Have a pint in Paudie's, the hotel pub, then take a leisurely walk around the town. Enjoy browsing the various shops or just drink in the beautiful scenery, then have a quiet dinner at one of the many great restaurants.

Dingle

Two pubs are on my "must go" list. The first is Murphy's, which is only a few establishments away from the hotel; it offers live entertainment and friendly service. The second, and my first choice because of its no-frills traditional Irish pub atmosphere, is O'Flaherty's, located on Bridge Street. The walls are lined with old posters, clippings, photos, and poems by local poets. Many years ago, I took a photo of two fine gentlemen having a pint of Guinness with the background of an old Guinness poster (see cover). On our next trip, I took copies of the photo to the pub owner, who made sure the men got the copies.

Since that trip, we have been corresponding with Tommy, the fine-looking gentleman in the gray sweater. Our last time in Dingle, Tommy was kind enough to pick us up at O'Flaherty's and take us to his home for a visit. Then he took us on a tour of Dingle Peninsula, ending with a pint at O'Flaherty's. This is just another example of the kindness of the Irish people. Most nights at O'Flaherty's, you'll find traditional Irish music performed by the owner, Fergus, his sister, and often patrons, along with an enthusiastic crowd.

Dingle

DAY SIX

The Beauty of Dingle

The scenery in the bay is breathtaking! The Johnny Cash song "Forty Shades of Green" can truly be appreciated looking at the hills surrounding Dingle.

One of the major attractions in Dingle is Fungie, a bottle-nosed dolphin. Fungie appeared in Dingle Harbour in 1984 and has been there ever since. If you are really adventurous and don't mind cold water, you can actually swim with Fungie, but I suggest taking the boat tour. It was raining, sometimes quite hard, the day we went out, but we had rain ponchos and still had a great time. The highlight of the trip is when Fungie emerges out of nowhere and swims parallel to the boat, actually slowing down at times so the boat can keep up. This is an adventure you will truly remember for a lifetime.

While in Dingle, be sure to plan your schedule to allow enough time to take an archaeological tour of the peninsula's breathtaking coastline. Also, another attraction of the tour is the stop at the Coumeenoole beach, the location of the filming of *Ryan's Daughter*. In my mind, it is one of the prettiest small beaches in Ireland. The movies *Far and Away* and *Leap Year* were partly filmed on the Dingle Peninsula. Spend the rest of the day exploring the streets of Dingle and enjoying a good dinner at one of its many restaurants. Anne tells me the hotel restaurant has some of the best mussels she has ever had, and I can vouch for the fish and chips. Have a pint or two at one of your favorite pubs (or find a new favorite) and plan to catch the bus in the morning for your next stop.

Coumeenoole Beach, Dingle

Gallarus Oratory, Dingle Archeological Tour

Another exceptional site is a trip to the Great Blasket Island. The island sits two miles off the mainland and is a short forty-minute ferry ride from Dingle. While uninhabited now, the population of the island was around a high of 175 in 1916 and a low of twenty-two in 1953 when the last inhabitants were evacuated by the government. Life was hard on the island, and the residents survived on fish from the sea, potatoes from the sparse land, and the few sheep they raised. In spite of the harsh living conditions, the island produced several prominent writers who chronicled their harsh existence and preserved the history for generations to come. You can enjoy the beach, walk the 1,100 acres of mountainous terrain, and explore the abandoned village. The ferry makes hourly trips, so you can spend as much or as little time as you wish.

DAY SEVEN

Experiencing Limerick

Today, catch the bus to Limerick. Although Limerick isn't a big tourist stop, some close-by sights are worth seeing. Again, I recommend the Jurys Inn in Limerick for its location and reasonable price. Take the afternoon you arrive there to explore. Have a pint at the Old Quarter pub. It is a little hard to find because of its location down what I would call an alley, but it's officially listed as being at 3 Little Ellen Street. It's a nice place to sit outside and enjoy the weather, watch people, and have a bite to eat if you are hungry.

Once rested up, take the short walk to King John's Castle. In 1210, King John of England ordered this castle built. It is well worth a look. Almost next door to the castle is the Hunt Museum, located in the eighteenth-century Old Custom House. It houses both ancient and modern treasures and is said to be one of the finest collections outside of Dublin. After exerting all the energy that sightseeing takes, it's time to cross the street to one of Limerick's oldest and most popular pubs, the Locke Bar, for a pint and dinner. You'll pass many pubs on the way back to the hotel, one of which is Flannery's. Flannery's, located at 17 Upper Denmark Street, is a quiet, comfortable pub where you can meet friendly locals who are willing to share their views on almost any subject, as long as the pints keep flowing.

DAY EIGHT

Bunratty Castle and Folk Park

Day eight will most likely prove to be one of your most enjoyable, with both historical and cultural significance. Catch a cab outside the hotel to Bunratty Castle and Folk Park. By now, I'm sure you have noticed I talk about buses, trains, or cabs instead of automobiles. If you are adventurous, you can rent a car and travel on your own schedule. Given the narrow roads and the driving on a different side of the road than we use in America, I would rather enjoy the ride than be hanging on for dear life while driving myself.

Bunratty Castle was built in 1425 on the O'Garney River and is a wonderful example of an authentic castle. Be sure to take the castle tour before moving on to the Bunratty Folk Park, which is a fantastic way to spend the day. From the moment you're on the grounds, it's an experience of sights, sounds, and smells. The green trees and plants, the roosters crowing, the smell of the peat burning in the fireplaces, and the cool fresh air all make you feel as if you have gone back in time. You will see individuals dressed in period garb who will explain the rules of the schoolhouse or what they are doing, like baking over the open fire or cutting and drying thatch. A replica of a nineteenth-century village features cottages and homes from various counties in Ireland that are rebuilt on the site, depicting the social positions and professions of the past owners. Examples are a fisherman's cottage, a farmhand's home, a landowner's home, and a working millhouse with a waterwheel operating the millstone. Throughout the grounds are many quiet paths and walkways, and you can easily spend most of the day and not see everything. This park is a "must do" every time we visit Ireland.

Bunratty Folk Park

Make sure you stop by Dirty Nellie's just outside the entrance of the park for a pint. Established in 1620, it was originally frequented by the castle guards and has become popular with both tourists and locals. After arriving back in Limerick, you can choose to eat at a number of places. One of our preferences is the Texas Steakhouse at 116 O'Connell Street. It is affordable and conveniently located, and it offers good food and a comfortable atmosphere.

The Jurys is a nice place to stay, but I would not recommend the restaurant for anything but breakfast; the pub is even more unimpressive.

DAY NINE

Adare Village

Catch a bus to the lovely, small village of Adare, which is nestled in the wooded countryside, its streets lined with small unique shops, thatch-covered cottages, and beautiful gardens. The famous Adare Manor, a five-star resort, is there, as well as its equally famous golf course. The Adare Heritage Center offers information on the history of the village and is a good place to start. A short walk down the road, you will find the ruins of a church that offers great photo opportunities. Actually, all of Ireland is a photo opportunity. After exploring the ruins, walk back to the city park. It's a great place to sit, relax, and enjoy the peacefulness of the area.

One of the things I appreciate most about Ireland is the slow pace of living, even in a city as big as Dublin. You can choose to have a pint and dinner in Adare, or you can catch the bus back to Limerick.

Bunratty Folk Park

DAY TEN

Back to Dublin

Have breakfast and choose to either explore more of Limerick or head to the train/bus station for your return trip back to Dublin. Buses leave approximately every hour. The station is an easy walk from the Jurys, or you can take a cab. If you would like to get back a little faster, you can also take the train, which departs per schedule. While bus travel is slower, I enjoy the scenery and getting to view some of the quaint small towns and villages that I would most likely not otherwise see. Don't be surprised if the bus stops at the entrance of someone's driveway in the countryside to pick up a passenger. It happened to us many times. I love the casual lifestyle of Ireland!

On one trip, our bus happened upon an auto accident that was going to keep the road closed for several hours. One of the passengers knew the area and directed the bus driver through some very narrow country roads and around the accident. That same passenger learned that a couple on the bus was going to miss its plane in Dublin due to the delay the accident caused. Her destination was the first stop in Dublin. She had the couple get off the bus with her, allowing her to drive the two to the airport in time to make their connection—Irish hospitality!

DAY ELEVEN

Kilmainham Gaol

Now that you have learned the history of the rebellion from the walking tour, it's time to see the Kilmainham Gaol. This is the jail where many of the political prisoners from the 1916 rebellion and the fight for Irish independence were incarcerated, tortured, and executed. Take the tour, listen to the commentary, and try to picture the bravery of those who put their lives on the line for what they believed in. After learning about the key players during this tour, take some time to browse the local bookstores to find at least one good resource on the 1916 Easter Rising. I'll guarantee you that it won't be a waste of time.

The gift shop at the jail also has several good publications on the jail and its history. Make sure you allow plenty of time to look around the museum in the jail; it contains numerous interesting items, including Michael Collins's publication supporting the treaty with Britain. You can get to the jail by walking, although it is a bit of walk. You also can take a cab or the "on and off" bus.

Kilmainham Gaol

After getting back to the city center, head up to 15 Suffolk Street to O'Donoghue's Pub for a pint and some chicken wings or their outstanding Irish beef stew. This is one of the few places where they actually wait on you at your table. Right across the street from O'Donoghue's is Pacino's, a really great Italian restaurant. I recommend trying their pizza, which is some of the best I have ever eaten. (There is another O'Donoghue's on Merrion Row that is known for its traditional music, but get there early for a seat).

If you are up for it, head over to Collage Street for a pint at Doyle's Pub. Doyle's has been a favorite of locals since 1977 and is a large but cozy pub and a great place for an afternoon pint. On your way back, stop by the Gaiety

Theater on South King Street, across from the Stephen's Green shopping center, to see what's playing. The Gaiety is an elegant, small theater that opened in 1871 and offers a variety of performances throughout the year. We have been fortunate to see *River Dance* there three times. If you decide to attend, plan on an early dinner, because most places stop serving meals before ten. Many of the restaurants around Dublin offer an early "theater menu."

DAY TWELVE

Glasnevin Cemetery

This morning, head over to the office of tourism and find out which city bus route takes you to the Glasnevin Cemetery. The bus costs almost nothing to ride, and if you have any questions about where to get off or where to catch it when you are ready to come back, the bus drivers and other passengers are more than willing to help. The Glasnevin Cemetery, founded in 1832, sits on 124 acres, and more than a million souls are buried in it. Glasnevin was the first cemetery that openly buried Catholics and Protestants alike. It was also one of the few that would bury stillborn babies on consecrated ground. The children are buried in an area of the cemetery called "Angels Plot." The older part of the cemetery is surrounded by high walls with watchtowers for armed guards that were built to prevent body snatchers from stealing bodies to sell for medical research.

Paupers and the famous alike are laid to rest here. One of the first gravesites you will notice is that of "The Liberator," Daniel O'Connell, who was the founder of the cemetery. The grave is marked by a massive round tower.

Among other people of importance buried at Glasnevin are Charles Parnell, Éamon de Valera, and Michael Collins. Some of the main characters of the movie *Michael Collins*, such as Harry Boland and Kitty Kieman, are buried here as well.

Glasnevin Cemetery

I recommend that everyone take the cemetery tour. The guides give the history of the cemetery and those buried there, and they tell interesting stories you wouldn't get on a self-guided tour. When leaving Glasnevin, turn left out of the gate and follow the sidewalk until the wall of the cemetery turns down an alley. Follow that alley to John Kavanagh's, a.k.a. Gravediggers Pub. Established in 1833 by John O'Neill, it's the oldest family pub in Dublin.

O'Neill turned the pub over to his son-in-law, John Kavanagh, in 1835. John and his wife had twenty-five children, three of whom served in the US Civil War. Upon returning from America, their son, Joseph, took over the pub.

Over the years, the pub has had many different family licensees and varying business success. Currently, the licensee is Eugene Kavanagh. The business is now in its sixth generation. We were lucky enough to meet Eugene, a fascinating and interesting gentleman with great enthusiasm for his work. He told us that the next two generations were working in his restaurant next door and that he hopes to pass the pub on to them. He even insisted on buying us a pint of Guinness after I told him it wasn't our favorite beer. He fervently explained that we couldn't truly appreciate Ireland without acquiring a taste for Guinness.

Our visit with Eugene was one of my highlights of our trip. Not much has changed with this pub in all those years—no music, no TV, and a musty aroma with furniture that appears to have been there since the pub opened. Just great atmosphere! The story has it that the gravediggers used to tap on the wall of the pub with their shovels for a drink, and the pub would secretly pass the drinks to the gravediggers through a small trapdoor in the wall of the pub that is shared with the cemetery, therefore allowing them to drink on the job. This pub is a must when visiting Dublin. Someone told me it is "hard to find, but harder to leave."

I suggest the Church Gallery bar and restaurant for dinner. The Church is just what the name implies. It is a church remodeled into a bar and restaurant located on Mary Street on the north side of Dublin. Get there early, have a pint at the bar, and take in the impressive architecture. They have an extensive menu, and we found the prices to be reasonable and the quality quite good.

DAY THIRTEEN

Waterford Day Trip

Today, catch the train from Dublin's Heuston Train Station for the two-and-a-half-hour trip to the historic town of Waterford. Viking raiders first established a settlement near Waterford in 853, making it what some consider Ireland's oldest city. The Vikings were driven out by the native Irish in 902, but reestablished in Waterford in 914. Throughout medieval time, Waterford was considered Ireland's "second city" after Dublin. When you arrive in Waterford, make sure you check the train schedule back to Dublin because it runs a limited number of times during the day.

Once you have your schedule, cross the bridge over the Suir River, turn left, and enjoy window-shopping as you walk down the street. A short distance down the street, you will find Reginald's Tower. The tower is the oldest civic building in Ireland and is believed to be the first to have mortar used in its construction.

Today, Waterford is known for Waterford Crystal. In 2008, we toured the Waterford Crystal factory, following the manufacturing from the molten crystal to the finished product. Watching craftsmen with more than twenty-five years' experience hand cutting the intricate designs from memory gives you a whole new appreciation for some of the finest crystal in the world. Unfortunately, the company went into receivership and closed in 2009. Waterford Crystal is now manufactured in the Czech Republic. At the request, or insistence, of Waterford City and the chamber of commerce, a new facility has been constructed near downtown, but it is only for demonstration purposes for tourists.

While exploring Waterford, you will come across a variety of places to lunch, shop, and have a pint. I encourage you to explore, while keeping one eye on your train schedule.

DAY FOURTEEN

A Bit of History

Spend the next few days getting to know Dublin. The city is rich in history, culture, and entertainment, and you will find endless ways to spend days, even weeks. Start the day off with a wonderful pastry at the Bakery, just down from the Jurys on Essex Street on the way to Temple Bar. Only two tables are inside, but a great outside seating area is located across the street.

In the same area as the Bakery is the National Photographic Archive. The archive houses some great historic photos of Ireland, and if you are looking for something in particular, you can use one of the research computers and then request the file you are interested in from the attendant. You can also order copies of any of the photos. We were able to purchase one of Michael Collins, Harry Boland, and Éamon de Valera all standing together. There are many interesting photos of Dublin and famous people before, during, and after the fight for independence.

One of the popular things to see while in Dublin is the *Book of Kells*. *The Book of Kells* gets its name from the Abbey of Kells in Kells, Ireland, where the book was housed for most of the medieval times. The book is printed on calf vellum and contains quality, vibrantly colored illustrations of humans, animals, Celtic knots, and the four gospels. Most believe it was written by Celtic monks in AD 800. In 1654, Cromwell housed his troops in the Abbey of Kells, so the governor of Kells sent the book to Dublin for safekeeping. In 1661, he presented it to Trinity College, where it has remained to this day. You most likely will stand in line for some time before getting to view it, but everyone visiting Dublin should see it, because many people consider it to be Ireland's finest national treasure.

Take time to walk around the town and note the architecture. The captivating, ornate buildings make Dublin a photographer's delight. The brightly colored doors of the houses are fascinating. One story of the reason for the colors is that when the queen of England died, England ordered the doors painted black to mourn the queen. The Irish, having no love for England, painted their doors bright colors in defiance. Another story is that wives painted each door a different bright color so that when their husbands came home from the pub, they could easily find the right house. As the title of this book implies, I rather like the second explanation. (Trouble is, the Jurys has glass doors.) Some of the best examples of these doors are on Merrion Street. Coming from St. Stephen's Green, walk up Merrion Row and make a left on Merrion Street.

At the corner of Merrion Row and Merrion Street is Foley's Pub. This was one of our favorites a few years ago, but the food quality has deteriorated, prices have gone up, and the service wasn't that outstanding. The corner pub is still a good place to have a pint, but I can't recommend the evening food, and I cannot comment on the upstairs restaurant either, because it's been some time since we've eaten there.

After a pint at Foley's, walk down Merrion Street. A little way down on the left, you'll find the National Museum, the National Gallery, the National History Museum, and the Leinster House, just to name a few. Across the street is Merrion Square, a good place to see Georgian architecture and the colorful entrances. You will find Merrion Square Park here. It is another great place to sit, relax, and people watch. A statue of Oscar Wilde sits on the northeast corner of the park. Dublin is known for its many famous authors, poets, and playwrights, including Oscar Wilde, Jonathan Swift, Bram Stoker, W. B. Yeats, and James Joyce. A writers' museum is located north of the Liffey on Parnell Square. I have been told it is an impressive museum, although I have never been there myself.

I mentioned Darwins restaurant previously, and when you're ready for dinner, this is the place to go. Located at 80 Aungier Street, it is by far our favorite restaurant. If I were rating on a scale of one to five, five being the best, I would rate Darwins a six. As a steak connoisseur, I can attest to the fact that they offer the best steaks in Ireland and use only certified Irish Angus beef. The menu also offers a wide variety of seafood and vegetarian dishes. As the name implies, the theme of the restaurant is based on Charles Darwin's *On the Origin of Species*. It is a small, nicely appointed restaurant with both great food and service. We were getting close to the end of our trip the first time we ate at Darwins and planned to eat there only once, but we ended up dining there four nights. The first night we met the owner, Dolores, and her daughter, Amy, who made us feel right at home. The second time we were there, every waiter came over to say hello, the bartender brought us a drink on the house, and Dolores brought out the chef to meet us. The last night, Dolores even sang at our table for us. We have not found a better restaurant, better food for the price, or better service anywhere in Ireland.

After dinner, cross to the other side of Aungier Street and follow it north toward Dame Street until you come to Fade Street and then turn right. About a half block down on the left side, you will see the Market Bar at 14A Fade Street. The Market Bar is in a large, old, factory building and is worth the price of a pint just to say you've been there. On your way back to the Jurys, walk down the north side of Dame Street to the Oak, which is made up of two parts: the older and smaller Oak at 81 Dame Street and the newer, larger, and more trendy pub, the Thomas Read, on Parliament Street. Stop in for a pint or two. Both of these are nice pubs to stop in for a drink, but they are nothing special compared to many others. That's true for most pubs, but if you don't try different ones, you won't find the real gems. Also, my gems may not be your gems, so explore.

DAY FIFTEEN

More History and a Little Shopping

Sleep in this morning, have breakfast in the hotel, then cross the street to the Christchurch. The first church was built on this site in 1038 from wood. The current structure dates back to the 1870s and is a magnificent example of the gorgeous, ornate stone structures of the time. Be sure to view the crypt, which is open to the public. To the west of the church, you will see a building with a banner advertising Dublinia, a historical recreation (living history) museum and visitor attraction that focuses on Dublin's Viking and Medieval history. It is said to be an accurate presentation of Dublin from 1170 to 1540. I guess it's okay, but I thought the displays were a bit cheesy.

Hungry? Head back across the street and around the corner from the Lord Edward to Burdock's Fish and Chips. Burdock's is a takeout "chipper" that uses fresh fish bought that morning and has the best chips in town. Chips are what we know as French fries, and crisps are potato chips. Visitors and locals alike love Burdock's. Mosey off toward the office of tourism and turn up Trinity Street from Dame, and have a pint at the Banker Pub.

The Banker is a small, intimate, friendly pub that makes you want to come back, or maybe not hurry to leave.

After your pint, or pints, wander the streets, browse the many shops, and maybe pick up that T-shirt or Irish treasure for your friends back home. Find a good place for dinner. Darwins always comes to my mind. After dinner, stop by the Long Hall Pub, which is coincidently just down from Darwins, and enjoy that last pint or two of the day.

DAY SIXTEEN

Traditional Irish Music

One pub we made a point of frequenting every Sunday afternoon we were in Dublin was the Brazen Head, Ireland's oldest pub, established in 1198. It has live music every night. From two to five every Sunday afternoon, one of the best Dublin traditional Irish music bands plays. We have been going to see them for years and never tire of listening to them. So let's pretend day sixteen is a Sunday. Get there early, around noon, so you can get a good seat, or you might find yourself standing most of your stay because the place fills up fast. You might want to grab a bite to eat before you go, or go early enough to eat before the band starts, because during the entertainment, they don't serve food in the room where the band performs. During the performance, many of the customers join the band for a song or two. You won't be listening long before you find yourself singing and swaying along with the rest of the bar to the more lively pub songs.

Don't be surprised if you end up sharing your table with fellow patrons, which makes the experience even more enjoyable. We have shared with people from Ireland, England, Scotland, and the United States, just to name a few. After the performance, stick around for dinner from the extensive, typical Irish menu. We've never had a bad meal, and the staff is friendly and efficient. The Brazen Head also has a good breakfast if you feel like getting there very early for the Sunday entertainment.

While there, look for the brochure about the "Evening of Food, Folklore, and Fairies." I will say more about this in the Day Twenty-Six section of this book, but you should definitely consider making plans to attend.

Brazen Head Pub

DAY SEVENTEEN

The Famine Ship

I recommend doing a couple of things between pub visits today. One of the touristy, but fun, things to do is take the Viking Splash Tour. The trip starts beside St. Stephen's Green on Merrion Row, where you'll board a World War II amphibious vehicle, don Viking helmets, and head off for a Viking adventure. The tour eventually ends up by "splashing" into the Grand Canal. The splash tour definitely will give you a different perspective from other tours you might take.

After the tour, stop into Neary's Pub for a pint. Neary's is just off Grafton Street on Chatham Street. It is a large, upscale pub, with lots of brass and wood. It's popular with the theater crowd and becomes busy late in the evening.

The second sight I recommend is the replica of the famine ship *Jeanie Johnston*. Cross over the Liffey and walk east on the sidewalk next to the Liffey. You'll come across a group of bronze statues depicting emaciated Irish emigrants during the famine. They are walking toward the ships on the docks that will take them out of Ireland. One million Irish died of disease and starvation, and another million left Ireland on ships like the *Jeanie Johnston* during the famine years of 1845 to 1849, only to die from the poor conditions onboard the ships. The conditions on these ships were so bad, and so many emigrants died on them, that they became known as "ghost ships." Stand facing the statues and slowly walk through them. Note their faces, the young child over the man's shoulders, the small bag of possessions, and the starving dog following them. I promise you will be moved by this haunting monument to those poor lost souls, the victims of oppression and starvation.

Famine Memorial

A short distance down the sidewalk you will find the *Jeanie Johnston*. You can see and take pictures of the

Jeanie from the sidewalk, but you really need to take the tour to get the real story of the ship. When you descend below deck and see the cramped quarters that at least 193 passengers shared for the forty-six average days the trip took, you understand how desperate these people were.

The original *Jeanie Johnston* took emigrants from Ireland to North America between 1847 and 1858. In all, the *Jeanie* carried more than 2,500 to North America and has the distinct honor of not having lost one passenger or crewmember. Many times, only one family member made the trip to North America with the hopes of getting a job and being able to send money home for fare for the rest of the family. Many never saw their family members again.

After this tour, head back to the south side and have a pint at the Hairy Lemon Pub on Stephen Street. The Hairy has great food, staff, and atmosphere. It is a popular spot with the student crowd, and the downstairs can become rather tight for space on weekend nights. The upstairs is much larger and a good place to enjoy a pint while watching the passersby on the street below. Either stay and enjoy the rest of the night or head over to Exchequer Street and the Old Stand Pub. The Stand has stood at its current location for more than three hundred years. It's a conventional, friendly pub with a more upscale interior. It is known for its hot lunches and fine wines.

DAY EIGHTEEN

Guinness Storehouse

As I mentioned earlier, Guinness beer is not one of my favorites, but many consider it a national treasure. You can spend much of a day at the Guinness Storehouse, which makes it today's sight to see. The Guinness storehouse is the number one paid tourist attraction in Dublin and worth the time and money.

To get there, turn left outside the Jurys and follow the road. It will change to Thomas Street. Then turn left from Thomas onto Crane Street. At the end of Crane, make a right onto Market Street. The Storehouse is on your right. It is about a ten-to-fifteen-minute walk, or you can take the hop-on, hop-off bus, a city bus, or a cab.

The Storehouse sits on the vast grounds of the Guinness brewery and is hard to miss from almost anywhere in Dublin. Its seven floors surround a glass atrium in the shape of a pint of Guinness. Each floor displays the history of Guinness, with the seventh floor housing the Gravity Bar, where you get a complimentary pint of Guinness and enjoy the 360-degree view of Dublin. It is truly a spectacular view.

The Guinness family has had a huge impact on Dublin—on all of Ireland, for that matter. Arthur Guinness signed a nine-hundred-year lease on the brewery, known as the St. James Gate Brewery, for just forty-five pounds per year in 1759, and it has stood at its current location since then. Arthur built housing for the employees, medical facilities, and a fire department. Over the years, the Guinness family has donated to the arts, built parks for the city, and restored more than one church. The generosity of the family cannot be overstated, and the people of Ireland show their appreciation by consuming more than a million pints a day.

On your way back, make a left on Bridge Street off of Thomas and walk two blocks. You will see the Liffey in front of you with one of my favorite pubs, the Brazen Head, on your left. On the right, across the street, is O'Shea's Merchant Pub. O'Shea's is a great place for a pint, decent food, and live entertainment. Its location gives you the option of staying there for dinner and the music or just having a pint or two and then going across the street to the Brazen Head. After you are done, it's a short, pleasant stroll back to the Jurys.

DAY NINETEEN

Shopping North of the Liffey

Take today to explore more of Dublin and plan a trip to Northern Ireland. Cross the O'Connell Bridge to the north side of the Liffey and follow O'Connell Street to Henry Street on your left. This is a good time to explore some of the stores along the way, and then take Henry to Moore Street.

On Moore Street is the Moore Street Market, where you will find vendors selling fresh vegetables, fruit, fish, homemade cheese, fresh breads, flowers, and almost anything else you can think of. It's very much like our farmers' markets, but on a much larger scale than I'm used to. Take time to inspect the wares and talk to both the vendors and customers. You can find out interesting tidbits about not only Dublin, but also Ireland as a whole. On weekends, you can also hit the Food Market at Temple Bar, close to the Jurys. It is much smaller than the Moore Street Market, but still a nice stop on your itinerary. After perusing the Moore Street Market, take a look around the indoor ILAC Shopping Center. You can enter from either Moore Street or Henry Street.

After your exhausting shopping spree, it's time to head over to Madigan's Pub. Not the Madigan's on North Earl Street, but the one at 16 Lower O'Connell Street. Like the "other" Madigan's on Earl, this is a casual pub with a friendly atmosphere. After a pint or two, head back to the south side of the Liffey, stop by the office of tourism, and pick up some information on Northern Ireland. There are many sights to see in Northern Ireland, and you can visit them safely now that the violence has subsided. I would avoid planning a stay during the popular July 12 parades. Parading is done mostly to assert a group's control over a particular area and can be controversial. Violent clashes have broken out shortly before, during, and after these parades, and I recommend that you avoid placing your-self in the path of possible harm. More on the causes of this violence later.

A window at the office of tourism just for Northern Ireland is a good place to get the information helpful in planning your trip. I suggest taking the train to Belfast, which leaves from Connolly Train Station daily. It is only a two-hour trip.

Northern Ireland is part of the United Kingdom and uses the British pound (£) instead of the euro (€) that the Republic of Ireland uses, so be sure to stop by the bank and exchange some of your currency into pounds before your trip. Northern Ireland establishments refuse to take or exchange euros for pounds. Even the banks won't exchange euros unless they have a "bureau of exchange" in their office. You can get pounds from ATM machines. An AIB bank is located on Dame Street on the way back to the Jurys. It has a money exchange, and the employees are friendly and helpful. I would exchange just what you think you will need for lunches on your side trips, tips, and a few pints; use a credit card for everything else. You seem to get the best exchange rate using a credit card.

After getting your information and picking up some literature about the North, head over to the Temple Bar area and the Temple Bar Pub, obviously named for the area in which it resides. Have a pint and make plans for the following day's adventures to the North.

A fun place for a traditional Irish dish for dinner and a pint is the famous and popular Oliver St. John Gogarty Pub, also in the Temple Bar area. You can't miss it; it's the four-story olive green and yellow pub on the corner of Fleet and Anglesea Streets. Traditional music sessions take place on most nights, as well as on weekends in the early afternoon. We happened to be there on July 4, and they did a fine job at an attempt to celebrate the US holiday of Independence Day, cowboy hats and all.

DAY TWENTY

The North: Belfast

As you travel to the North, you will most likely want to take a cab to the train station because of your luggage and the distance from the Jurys. Remember, the train to Belfast leaves from Connolly Train Station. The two major train stations in Dublin are the Connolly and Heuston Train Stations, and the cab driver will ask which you are headed to. If you don't remember, just tell the driver your destination, and he'll get you to the right station.

You'll find yourself engrossed in the verdant countryside, and the two-hour trip will fly by. Once you get to Belfast, catch a cab to your hotel. We suggest the Europa Hotel; although expensive, it is in a fine location for sightseeing. It is best to make advance reservations. The Europa has the dubious honor of being one of the most bombed hotels in Europe. It was a popular target of the IRA during the height of unrest in Northern Ireland because of its popularity with foreign dignitaries as a place to stay.

Irish Countryside

Belfast became known as home to one of the largest shipyards in the world. The shipyards are best known for the *Titanic* being built there in 1912 by Harland and Wolff, which remains one of the largest shipbuilders to this day. Also impressive are the two giant shipbuilding cranes known as Samson and Goliath, which dominate the Belfast skyline.

Speaking of the *Titanic*, her last port of call was on the south coast of County Cork in the small town of Cobh. If you get a chance, take a trip there. Cobh is also the location where many of the survivors and victims of the *Lusitania* were brought. It is a quaint seaside town with an emotionally moving history. In Cobh, you will find a statue of Annie Moore. Annie, at fifteen years old and traveling with her nine- and eleven-year-old brothers, became the first Irish immigrant to pass through Ellis Island in New York Bay on January 1, 1892. She was given a ten-dollar gold piece for being the first to cross the threshold. The three were reunited with her parents, who were already in America. The song "Isle of Hope, Isle of Tears" captures Annie's experience.

Cobh

Take the rest of the day to get your bearings. Make sure you take the time to set up your Black Taxi tour for the next day. This tour is a "must do" for anyone wanting a better understanding of Northern Ireland and the complex issues that still cause unrest within the North. This would also be a good time to set up a tour to

Carrick-a-Rede and the Giant's Causeway. Both are must-see attractions when in the North.

Once you have booked your tours, if you are feeling somewhat parched, cross the street from the Europa to the Crown Pub. The Crown's exterior is beautiful, but the inside is exquisite, with its nooks, crannies, rooms, and ornate woodwork. This is a nice place to unwind, have a pint, and have either a light "pub food" dinner or a full-blown meal.

DAY TWENTY-ONE

Black Taxi Tour

Before you take the Black Taxi tour, there are some things you should understand about the North. Belfast became the center of the secular conflict between Roman Catholic and Protestant citizens. These two groups are also referred to as Nationalist and Unionist or Republican and Loyalist. The conflict is really about the rule of the North, with the Nationalists wanting to become part of the Republic of Ireland and the Unionists wanting to remain under Britain. Between 1969 and the late 1990s, Belfast saw some of the worst violence in recent history; it became known as "the Troubles." The city is still divided by a wall, with the Catholics on one side and the Protestants on the other. The city center is considered neutral territory. Even the schools are segregated by Catholic and Protestant, and although the violence now seems to be confined to the time the parades are held, the hatred and distrust still run deep.

The Black Taxi tour company employs both Catholic and Protestant drivers. You will be taken to neighborhoods on both sides of the wall and to the famous, but disturbing, murals painted on the ends of row houses depicting the North's troubled past. I suggest that you take the tour twice—once with a Catholic driver and once with a Protestant driver. You will see the same things, but the drivers' perspectives of the cause of the trouble will be polar opposites. I asked our Protestant driver if he had any Catholic friends and if they ever got together for a pint; he bristled and said, "Absolutely not!" He told me there's not a family in Belfast that hasn't been affected, by having a family member or friend arrested, maimed, or killed because of the violence. He told me the drivers say they are friends but that they don't trust each other and don't socialize with those outside their religion.

We've noticed that the people of the North are not nearly as friendly and open as those in the republic. I believe it comes from that distrust and having to live with those feelings every day of their lives. The people don't have a problem with tourists, but if you are Irish, you are pretty much expected to pick a side. I spoke to several people from the republic who don't visit the North because of the tension that still exists.

Back from our tour, we opted to go to a great place for a pint and a bite to eat: Laverys Pub at 12–18 Bradbury Place. Laverys is a short walk from the hotel and is the oldest family-owned pub in Belfast. Prior to our trip North, a bartender in Dublin asked us what we were going to see while in Ireland. When we told him we were going to Belfast, he told us about Laverys. He gave us a note to give to one of the bartenders; it told the man he should buy us a pint, which he did. The gentleman actually sat and visited with us for some time and checked in with us several times to make sure we were being cared for. The food is excellent, prices are reasonable, service is great, and the entertainment will keep you late into the night.

DAY TWENTY-TWO

Giant's Causeway

Make sure your camera batteries are charged for your sightseeing adventure to two of the most picturesque and unusual sights in Ireland: Carrick-a-Rede and Giant's Causeway. It is a good idea to hire a private driver for this tour so that you can set your own pace; the motor coach tours also do an acceptable job.

You will make several stops along the way, but the first main attraction on the tour is Carrick-a-Rede, which means "rock in the road." Carrick-a-Rede is a rope suspension bridge that was originally put up each spring to allow access from the mainland to the rich salmon fishing on the small island the bridge connects to. Now it is mostly a tourist attraction. On an ordinary day, the walk across the bridge is spectacular and breathtaking, but the day we were there, the wind was blowing so hard that the rain was horizontal and felt like pebbles hitting us. By the time I got to the bridge, I was soaking wet. You may have noticed I changed from "we" to "I." Anne chose to stay at the visitors' center because she is not one to tempt fate by exploring high places, even in the best weather conditions. The bridge was swaying in the wind and slippery with rain, which made the crossing even more spectacular. The photo opportunities from the bridge—left, right, and down—can't be described. If you told me the only way I could cross it again would be under the same conditions, I would still be the first in line for the crossing!

Most likely, your next stop will be the village of Ballintoy. Ballintoy is one of those places that make you think you're standing in a scene from a postcard. The view of the coastline with its white foam surf, the rugged shore, and the scent of the fresh sea air will take your breath away. A comfortable place for a pint, lunch, and a conversation with locals is the Fullerton Arms Pub. One of the patrons told me he lived just a few minutes from the Carrick-a Rede and hadn't been across it in years. Looking like a drowned rat after my rainy walk, he laughed, looked up at the sky, and told me the rain would stop in about an hour. Guess what? Almost to the minute, the rain stopped in an hour. Of course, when in Ireland, you have to remember that if it isn't raining, it will be, and if it is, it most likely won't be for long. A gentleman told me that a smart Irishman isn't the one who takes his umbrella when it is raining, but the one who takes it when it isn't.

Another stop you will most likely make if you are on a tour will be Bushmills and the Old Bushmills Distillery. Everyone knows of Bushmills whiskey. Although distilleries aren't high on my list of things to see, most of the people seemed to enjoy the stop and the sample they received at the end of the distillery tour. Another great photo opportunity along the way is Dunluce Castle, which is perched on the cliffs and an imposing sight. Unfortunately, we didn't get time to explore the castle, but just the view from the road makes for some great photographs. Ireland has no shortage of castle ruins, but this one looks to be worth a trip back to take a closer look.

After arriving at the visitors' center of the Giant's Causeway, you will need to catch the shuttle bus down to the shoreline. Although the scientific explanation for the forty thousand-plus interlocking stone columns is volcanic activity some fifty million years ago, I prefer the more colorful explanation of Irish folklore. Legend has it that the causeway was built by Finn McCool as a walkway to Scotland to fight the Scottish giant, Benandonner (hence *Giant's* Causeway). After awaking from a nap, Finn saw Benandonner appear on the horizon and realized how much larger Benandonner was than he was. Finn ran to his wife, Oonagh, for suggestions on what he should do. Oonagh quickly devised a plan and then disguised Finn as a baby. Next, she had him get into a huge cradle and pretend to be asleep. When Benandonner saw how imposing the "child's" size was, he began to worry about the size of Finn, the father. The giant then turned around and returned to Scotland, destroying the walkway as he went. This certainly makes more sense than a volcano, doesn't it? Be sure to look for a rock formation that resembles a chair. This is known as the wishing chair. As the myth goes, all wishes made while setting in the chair come true.

Giant's Causeway

DAY TWENTY-THREE

Back to Dublin

Catch the train back to Dublin today, and take the time to investigate places I haven't told you about. The best part of Ireland is finding those hidden gems off the beaten path and not in the tourist books.

Dunluca Castle

DAY TWENTY-FOUR

South of the Grand Canal

Head over to the office of tourism and set up one of the several available day trips to the Wicklow Mountains for the next day; then continue your exploration of Dublin. Several distinctive neighborhoods in and around Dublin are worth visiting, each with unique qualities and attractions. By now, if you have followed the suggestions in this book, you are undoubtedly intimately familiar with the Temple Bar area and have seen Merrion Square with its colorful doors and beautiful Georgian architecture. Take some time to stroll south of the Grand Canal to the Ballsbridge-Embassy Row neighborhood. With its grass yards, tree-lined streets, and upscale residences and foreign embassies, it's a pleasant place to spend an afternoon. This area is also home to several high-end hotels and restaurants.

Later, head back to Grafton, Dawson, and Kildare Streets for dinner at one of the many interesting restaurants in the area. After dinner, a nice place for a pint or two is the Duke bar, 8–9 Duke Street, just off Grafton. The

Duke has plenty of room, and the staff and patrons are vivacious and friendly.

Another pub you might want to amble, or stagger, over to is Auld Dubliner at 24–25 Temple Bar. The Auld is a lively, traditional Irish pub with live music upstairs most days. As you might expect from a Temple Bar-area pub, the place is an attraction to tourists but also has its share of locals. The Auld is a fun place to spend the evening, but be warned that it can and does become so boisterous that not only can't you have a conversation, you can't hear yourself think. The Temple Bar area is always an entertaining place for "people watching." In fact, we actually ordered a pitcher of margaritas from one of the pubs late one night, sat at a small outside table, and watched the sea of people hop from pub to pub. It's also a very popular area for hen parties, the Irish equivalent to our bachelorette parties. You are likely to see unusual dress and witness some interesting behavior.

DAY TWENTY-FIVE

Glendalough Day Trip

Today, catch your tour to the Wicklow Mountains. Something to watch for on your trip to the mountains, or any of your side trips for that matter, are fairy rings. In Irish folklore, fairy rings are circles, or rings, of mushrooms or mounds of grass where fairies have been dancing. A favorite resting place for fairies is under a hawthorn tree, and that is how you will identify them. You will notice cultivated fields that have areas of shrubs with a tree in the middle. Farmers believe these areas to be fairy rings; they fear the wrath of the fairies if they clear them. While no one will admit that they really believe in fairies, the story goes that a major highway construction path was diverted to avoid cutting down a hawthorn tree.

The legend of fairies is both fascinating and entertaining. If you want to learn more, numerous Internet sites are devoted to the subject. Better yet, attend the "Evening of Food, Folklore, and Fairies" discussed on Day Twenty-Six.

At least one tour takes you through Rathdrum. Rathdrum Square was a location in the movie *Michael Collins,* where Michael was speaking to a crowd in support of a free Ireland. Several scenes were filmed in the upstairs part of Woodpack Pub. The assassination of Michael was filmed near the town of Bray.

Another tour will take you to the town of Kilkenny for a few hours, with the option of exploring Dunmore Caves before heading to the Wicklow Mountains. Kilkenny is a medieval city located on the banks of the River Nore and is steeped in both history and legends. One of the first things you will notice as you enter the city is the stately Kilkenny Castle sitting high above the river. Kilkenny was the possession of a son-in-law of Strongbow and later the Earl of Ormond. Kilkenny was the site of many parliaments, one of which enacted the Statute of Kilkenny in 1366. This statute made marriage between a Norman and an Irishwoman an act of high treason. Irishmen were also not allowed to live within the walls of the city. As through much of Irish history, the Irish were used, abused, and mistreated in their own country. They were not allowed to be educated, own land, or practice their religion as recently as the early 1900s.

You'll also hear of the "Witch of Kilkenny," whose name was Alice Kyteler. Alice was born into a noble Kilkenny family in 1280. She was married four times, and each husband died. After the death of her last husband, Alice's children accused her of using sorcery to kill him. Bishop Richard de Ledrede investigated the children's accusations and determined that Alice was indeed a witch. The bishop then wrote to Roger Outlawe, the chancellor of Ireland, requesting that Alice be arrested. Unfortunately for the bishop, the chancellor was Alice's brother-in-law and would not have her arrested. To make it worse for the bishop, another of Alice's brother-in-laws arrested the bishop and had him thrown in prison. After only a few weeks, the bishop was released. The bishop continued on his relentless crusade to have Alice tried for heresy. Eventually, Alice fled to England and never returned. Alice escaped the bishop, but her maidservant was not so lucky. The bishop accused the maid, Petronella de Meath, of heresy and had her flogged and burned at the stake in 1324. Petronella holds the regrettable distinction of being the first person to be burned at the stake in Ireland.

If you chose to spend less time in Kilkenny and take the tour of the Dunmore Caves, please note that you will need to navigate more than three hundred steps during the short tour, but if you are physically able, you won't be sorry.

The Wicklow Mountains and the surrounding areas have been featured in numerous movies such as *Michael*

Collins, Excalibur, and *PS I Love You.* You'll likely make a stop to see the Sally Gap, filmed in the movie *Braveheart.*

The main stop on your tour will be the sixth-century monastery founded by Saint Kevin. The monastery is located at Glendalough, or "Glen of the Two Lakes." The site held many treasures and was the target of numerous raids by the Vikings in the ninth and tenth centuries and the English in the fourteenth century. Even with the relentless attacks, the monastery remained in use until the sixteenth century. Take time to wander the grounds and note the unique crosses and the building's remains. Take special note of the roof on the small stone chapel. Then picture having the ability to build a completely stone roof and have it last hundreds of years; it's truly amazing. If time and weather permit, walk the path along the lake and enjoy the peacefulness that makes one realize why people were drawn to this location.

Glendalough

Some tours will make a stop in the small town of Avoca. (Others will make a direct return to Dublin.) Avoca is best known for the Handweavers company and Ireland's oldest working woolen mill. Although I could pass on the weaving exhibit, a stroll around the town and the banks of the river is relaxing.

You will return to Dublin early enough for a short nap or a few pints before dinner. If you choose the latter, an enjoyable place is the Porterhouse Pub. There are no fewer than three Porterhouses in Dublin, and all are equally fine microbreweries with a pleasant atmosphere; lots of dark, heavy wood; and a variety of finely crafted beers, lagers, and seasonal selections. They also have tempting menus that just might entice you to stay for dinner and a pint or two more.

DAY TWENTY-SIX

Exploring the "Old City"

Sleep in today, have a full Irish breakfast, and head off on foot to explore the "Old City." Medieval Dublin was a walled city, with the castle at the center. Those living within the walls paid taxes to the castle in return for the protection of the walls. The wall started just west of Bridge Street and extended along the Liffey River east to Parliament Street, then south to Ship Street. From Ship, it extended southeast to Nicholas Street, then northwest down Lamb Alley back to the Liffey. A wall extended from Bridge Street and east down Cook Street to Exchange Street because that was where the River Liffey flowed at high tide.

From the front of the hotel, cross the street, turn left (west), and walk to Upper Bridge Street. At the corner of Bridge and Cornmarket, you will find St. Audoen's Church. Founded in 1190, it is Dublin's oldest parish still in use. Parts of the wall still exist, one section being the north wall on the grounds of St. Audoen's that parallels Cook Street, so named because food vendors would place their cooking fires outside the walls for fear of fires inside the walls. Standing at the top of the wall gives you a feel for the original height of the battlements. For a few euros, you can tour the inside of the church. After completing your time at the church, go back to the corner where you began, cross the street, and take a closer look at the portion of the surviving wall standing at Cornmarket and Lamb Alley. Walk back in the direction you started from this morning (east) and turn right on Nicholas Street. Follow Nicholas to St. Patrick's Cathedral, which was built next to a well that is said to be where Saint Patrick baptized converts around AD 450. The original church was built with wood and rebuilt from stone somewhere around 1192. Much of the current structure dates back to 1250 to 1270.

When you have seen the cathedral, head east on Bull Alley (on the north side of the grounds), which changes to Golden Lane, Upper Stephen Street, then Lower Stephen Street. Follow Lower Stephen to William Street South. Turn left on William Street, and just past Coppinger Row you will see Powerscourt Townhouse Centre. Powerscourt was the townhouse of a famous Georgian family that has been converted into one of Dublin's most distinctive shopping centers. You also can reach Powerscourt from Grafton Street down the narrow Johnson Court Alley. You will find no mainstream stores here, just unique craft shops, art galleries, snack and wine bars, and restaurants. It has a lovely sky-lit courtyard that is a great place to have a quick bite for lunch.

After leaving Powerscourt, continue down William Street South to St. Andrew's Street. At the end of St. Andrew's, you will find Suffolk Street and the office of tourism. Head north to College Green and turn left. College Green will turn into Dame Street. Make sure you are on the south side of Dame Street. Watch the sidewalk for a mosaic with the picture of a stag and an arrow pointing down a narrow passageway. That passageway will lead you to Dame Court and the Stag's Head Pub, which is known for its beautiful Victorian interior. I recommend a visit to this pub during the day or very early evening because it is a popular hangout for the younger crowd at night. If you don't like the feeling of being a sardine in a can, you can find more comfortable places to enjoy the evening.

This would be a good night to attend the "Evening of Food, Folklore, and Fairies" night I mentioned previously. The folklore night is held in a room upstairs at the Brazen Head; reservations are required. The meal is tasty, and the narrator, Johnny Daly, makes the night light, interesting, and informative. The presentation includes the history of the Irish people, how they lived, and how storytelling was an intricate part of Irish life. It then goes into the otherworld of the fairies. You will learn about the different types of fairies, fairy rings, how the stories of fairies were used to teach lessons to both young and old, and how the beliefs survived in Ireland when they were lost in so many other places. It is a truly magical evening that is near the top of my "must do" list.

DAY TWENTY-SEVEN

Cong and Athlone

Two places we feel you should not miss if you have the time are Cong, where *The Quiet Man* starring John Wayne was filmed, and Kylemore Abbey. It takes a little preplanning if you're not driving. We made hotel reservations online to spend the night in Athlone and made arrangements with Mary O'Grady to meet us at the train station there, which is about a two-hour trip from Dublin's Heuston Train Station. While we used Mary, I'm sure you could make plans at the office of tourism or wait until you get to Athlone and check with its office of tourism. Not being one to wing it, I preferred the assurance of having Mary waiting for us. The handy thing about having someone like Mary is that she will get you there, let you explore at your own pace, and be waiting to take you to your next destination.

After checking into your hotel, head off to the small town of Cong, which is best known for being the filming location of the movie *The Quiet Man*. The actual set used in the pub scenes of the film is in the Pat Cohan Pub. It is a pleasant place to enjoy a pint and check out the photos from the movie. The best parts of Cong are its picturesque forest, the medieval Royal Abbey ruins, and the monk's fishing house, which sits over the Cong River and has a hole in the floor that the monks could fish through. It is believed that a line ran from the house to a bell in the monastery that allowed the monks to let the cook know if they would be having fish for dinner. A walk through the forest is one of the most relaxing times you will spend in Ireland.

Monk's Fishing House, Cong

After you've had your fill of Cong, it's off to Kylemore Abbey, which has a picture-postcard setting and is truly worth the stop for the view alone. Construction of the abbey started in 1867 and took more than one hundred workers four years to finish. It was built as a private home for Mitchell Henry, a doctor from London, who sold it to the duke and duchess of Manchester in 1909. After living in the home for several years, the duke and duchess had to sell it due to gambling debts. In 1920, the Irish Benedictine nuns purchased the abbey after being forced out of Belgium during World War I. The nuns ran a girls' school at the abbey until they had to close it in 2010.

The abbey sits on a thousand acres and has a beautiful walled Victorian garden. A short walk along the *lough* will take you to a lovely Gothic church. The word *lough* is pronounced "loch" and comes from the Irish *loch*, meaning "lake."

Kylemore Abbey

If time permits, take a short drive through the small, quaint town of Clifden on your way back to Athlone. If you have a driver, you will need him or her only to get you back to Athlone; from there you can do things on your own. When you leave tomorrow, the train station is only a short walk. Once back, wander the streets of Athlone.

Athlone is positioned in the central part of Ireland and has always been a major crossing point over the Shannon River, which runs through the heart of the town. It has been the site of many battles for control of the river crossing over the years, and because of its strategic importance, the Athlon Castle was built in 1210 to defend that crossing point. Today, one of the first things you notice is the well-preserved Athlone Castle. It rests on the banks of the Shannon at the one bridge that connects the two sides of the town.

I suggest that you eat early; we found it hard to find a restaurant that stayed open late. If you walk to the opposite side of the Shannon from Athlone Castle, which is the side your hotel is most likely on, you will find Strand Street close to the river's edge. Strand Street has an excellent restaurant called Hatters Lane Bistro. Both the service and food are exquisite. They offer some tasty daily specials, and prices are reasonable. After dinner, you can either do more sightseeing or have a pint or two and save the sightseeing for tomorrow. Just up the hill from Hatters Lane Bistro, you will find Gertie Brownes Pub, a typical local Irish pub with friendly staff. Gertie's is a quiet place to unwind after your long day of exploring.

Gertie Brown Pub

DAY TWENTY-EIGHT

Back to Dublin

In the morning, check out of your hotel and head out for shopping, a stroll around the town or along the river, or take the Viking river cruise on the Shannon for some history of the area and the lovely scenery. It rained the day we took the cruise, but we still enjoyed it immensely. You will have more than enough time to see Athlone's sights because the train leaves approximately every two hours late into the evening. We chose to return to Dublin in the early evening so that we could have dinner and a pint at one of our favorites, but you could choose to stay in Athlone for dinner and then head back to Dublin.

DAY TWENTY-NINE

DART and the Irish Sea

If you have good weather today, take the day to ride the Dublin Area Rapid Transit (DART). Follow the sidewalk along the Liffey east to the Tara Street DART station. Buy the pass that allows you to hop on and off all day. The DART runs north and south along the Irish Sea and stops at several small towns and villages along the way. I recommend three stops that are worth taking the time to see.

The first is Dalkey, which is on the south route of DART. Take a walk around this inviting little town and take the tour of the Dalkey Castle. The guides are in period dress and stay in character while describing what you are seeing. It's both entertaining and informative.

My second recommendation, also south, is Bray. You will see Bray from the window even before it is announced because of the large Ferris wheel and carnival-like rides along the shore. Bray is a beautiful seaside town that deserves a little of your time to explore. Bray and the surrounding area have been featured in many movies.

My third recommendation is north of Dublin and almost at the end of the DART line. It's the small fishing and yachting village of Howth. Step out of the Howth Train Station and you will see the Bloody Stream Pub under it. Pop in and have a pint and a sandwich before venturing off to drink in the beauty of Howth. Take a walk around the corner and down the dock to explore the many fish markets with an amazing variety of fresh seafood. Just outside the markets, you can watch the seals begging for a handout and see many of the boats in the working fishing fleet. At the end of the pier is the Howth lighthouse. After visiting the docks, stroll down the main street and appreciate the sea air and the beauty of the harbor. At the end of the street is a little store where you can get a soft ice cream cone. Then walk along the levy and watch the fishermen in their small boats pulling in their lobster traps. Note the homes on the side of the hill to your right and picture the view they must have. You can certainly see why someone would want to live in Howth. Go back a block or two and go up the hill past the old church ruins to the Abbey Tavern for a pint. The abbey is listed in most guidebooks as one of the top pubs in Ireland, and I would have to agree that it is right up there with some of the best. It has a rich, warm, dark wood interior with the bar in the center and tables around the outside perimeter. It has a cozy feel that makes it an inviting place to relax, discuss your day's adventures, and plan your next one. After leaving the abbey, stop by the Waterside Pub on Harbour

Road. Sit in the front where the windows are pulled open, and you can enjoy the fresh sea breeze and do a little more people watching.

You can get back on the DART and head back to Dublin or stop at one of the many other places along the way. I have mentioned only three, but there are many interesting stops, especially on the south route.

DAY THIRTY

Rebel Walking Tour

As this is your last day in Ireland, pack what you can, check your airline reservations, and if you have a lot of luggage, make arrangements to have a cab big enough to handle it waiting for you in the morning. There are always plenty of cabs outside the hotel, but most are compact cars and can't accommodate a large amount of luggage.

Head across the River Liffey on O'Connell Street to Parnell and make a left. Go a short distance, then turn left on Parnell Square. Just past the corner is the Sinn Féin Bookshop at 58 Parnell Square. This is where you catch the start of the Rebel Walking Tour that covers the 1916 Easter Rising after the rebels left the GPO. It is a fantastic follow-up to the previous 1916 Rebellion tour I wrote about in Day Three. I recommend taking this tour after the 1916 Rebellion tour. It is given most days, but make sure you check ahead of time. We found that most people didn't know about this tour, including the office of tourism, so the best way is to actually go to the bookshop earlier to find the schedule. We found out about it from a Peadar Kearney bartender.

In this tour, you will see the building used as both the headquarters of the rebels and one of the boardinghouses used by Michael Collins. You'll make a stop at the enchanting Garden of Remembrance. The garden is located on the corner on Parnell Square North and Parnell Square East and is dedicated to "all those who gave their lives in the cause of Irish freedom." A plaque has the following inscription on it:

In the darkness we saw a vision.

We lit the light of hope and it was not extinguished.

In the desert of discouragement we saw a vision.

We planted a tree of valour and it blossomed.

In the winter of bondage we saw a vision.

We melted the snow of lethargy and the river of resurrection flowed from it.

We sent our vision aswim like a swan on the river. The vision became a reality.

Winter became summer. Bondage became freedom and this we left to you as your inheritance.

O generations of freedom remember us, the generations of the vision.

As you move south to O'Connell, you will find yourself at a monument of Charles Stewart Parnell. There you will discuss the Easter Uprising and the activities that happened in the GPO. I think the best part of the tour is from this point on. The guide will take you down the byways and side streets as the rebels did as they tried to escape. His description will make you feel like you should be ducking bullets as you walk down the narrow streets. You'll see a plaque that reads,

> Written after I was shot. Darling Nancy I was shot leading a rush up Moore Street and took refuse in a doorway. While I was there I heard the men pointing out where I was and made a bolt for the laneway I am in now. I got more than one bullet I think. Tons and tons of love dearie to you and the boys and to Nell and Anna. It was a good fight anyhow. Please deliver this to Nannie O'Rahilly, 40 Herbert Park, Dublin. Goodbye Darling.

Michael O'Rahilly wrote these words to his wife on the back of a letter from his son he had received while fighting from the GPO. The enemy left him dying and begging for water for hours.

After the tour, head back to the south side of the Liffey and go east to 35 Sir John Rogerson's Quay and the Ferryman, a hotel and pub. The Ferryman is right next to the Samuel Beckett Bridge, the one that looks like a harp. The Ferryman offers a lunch carvery Monday through Friday and is a nice place for a quiet lunch and a cold pint.

This is also a good day to visit some of your favorite sights and pubs and say good-bye to new acquaintances and old friends. We always try to make a last visit to St. Stephen's Green and have a pint at Peadar Kearney's.

A good way to spend your last night is at Johnnie Fox's "Hooley Night." Johnnie Fox's was established in 1798 and is located in the Dublin Mountains, around thirty minutes from Dublin. It is known as the highest pub in Ireland. You can go for just dinner or a pint, but I think everyone should experience Hooley Nights once. You most likely will have to make reservations before attending because it seems to always be crowded. The cost includes dinner and a night of entertainment, from music to Irish dancing.

An express bus leaves from several locations around Dublin and returns a short time after the show for a very reasonable price each way. The building and the interior decor of Johnnie Fox's make your visit well worth the time. Another big plus is that you can get back to your room early enough to avoid interfering with an early-morning departure.

"THE" FIFTY PUBS

1. O'Neills
   #2 Suffolk Street, Dublin

2. Bull & Castle
   #5–7 Lord Edward Street, Dublin

3. Lord Edward
   #23 Christchurch Place, Dublin

4. Peadar Kearney's
   #64 Dame Street, Dublin

5. The Quays
   #12 Temple Bar, Dublin

6. International Bar
   #23 Wicklow Street, Dublin

7. The Oval
   #78 Abbey Street, Dublin

8. Madigans
   #25 North Earl Street, Dublin

9. Dawson Lounge
    #25 Dawson Street, Dublin

10. O'Donoghue's Pub
    #15 Suffolk Street, Dublin

11. O'Donoghue's
    #15 Merrion Row, Dublin

12. Doyle's Pub
    #9 College Street, Dublin

13. John Kavanagh's aka Gravediggers
    #1 Prospect Square, Dublin

14. The Church Gallery Bar
    Corner of Jervis and Mary Street, Dublin

15. Foley's Pub
    #1 Merrion Row

16. Market Bar
    #14A Fade Street, Dublin

17. The Oak
    #81 Dame Street, Dublin

18. Thomas Read
    #1 Parliament Street, Dublin

19. The Banker Pub
#16 Trinity Street, Dublin

20. The Long Hall Pub
#51 South George Street, Dublin

21. Brazen Head
#20 Lower Bridge Street, Dublin

22. Neary's Pub
#1 Chatham Street, Dublin

23. Hairy Lemon
#41–42 Stephen Street, Dublin

24. The Old Stand
#37 Exchequer Street, Dublin

25. O'Shere Merchant Pub
#12 Lower Bridge Street, Dublin

26. Madigan's Pub
#16 Lower O'Connell Street, Dublin

27. Madigan's Pub
#25 North Earl Street, Dublin

28. Temple Bar
#47–48 Temple Bar, Dublin

29. **Oliver St. John Gogarty Pub**
   #54–59 Fleet Street, Dublin

30. **Duke Pub**
   #9 Duke Street, Dublin

31. **Auld Dubliner**
   #24–25 Temple Bar, Dublin

32. **Porterhouse Pub**
   #16–18 Parliament Street, Dublin

33. **Stag's Head Pub**
   #1 Dame Ct., Dublin

34. **Ferryman's**
   #35 Sir John Rogerson Quay, Dublin

35. **Johnnie Fox's**
   Glencullen, Dublin

36. **Paudie's**
   Strand Street, Dingle

37. **Murphy's**
   Strand Street, Dingle

38. **O'Flaherty's**
   Bridge Street, Dingle

39. Old Quarter Pub
     #3 Little Ellen Street, Limerick

40. The Locke Bar
     #2A Georges Quay, Limerick

41. Flannery's
     #17 Upper Denmark Street, Limerick

42. Dirty Nellie's
     Bunratty Castle, Limerick

43. Crown Pub
     #49 Great Victoria Street, Belfast

44. Lavery's Pub
     #12–18 Brodbury Place, Belfast

45. Fullerton Arms Pub
     Ballintoy Village

46. Pat Cohan Pub
     Cong

47. Gertie Brownes
     #9 Costume Place, Athlone

48. Bloody Stream
     Railway Station, Howth

49. Abbey Tavern
    #28 Abbey Street, Howth

50. Waterside Pub
    Harbour Road, Howth

FAVORITES

Athlone

Pub

Gertie Brownes — Day Twenty-Seven

For Dinner

Hatters Lane — Day Twenty-Seven

Belfast

Hotel

Europa — Day Twenty

Pubs

The Crown — Day Twenty

Laverys Pub — Day Twenty-One

For Lunch

Fullerton Arms (way to Giant's Causeway) — Day Twenty-Two

For Dinner

Laverys Pub — Day Twenty-One

Sights

Black Cab tour — Days Twenty & Twenty-One

Giant's Causeway — Days Twenty & Twenty-Two

Carrick-a-Rede — Days Twenty & Twenty-Two

Cong

Pub

Pat Cohan	Day Twenty-Seven

Sights

Royal Abbey	Day Twenty-Seven

Dingle

Hotel

Dingle Bay Hotel	Day Five

Pubs

O'Flaherty's	Day Five
Murphy's	Day Five

Dinner

Dingle Bay Hotel	Day Five

Sights

Fungie the Dolphin	Day Six
Archaeological tour	Day Six

Dublin

Hotel

Jurys Christchurch	Day One

Pubs

Peadar Kearney's	Day Two
The Brazen Head	Days Sixteen & Eighteen
Gravediggers	Day Twelve
O'Neills	Day One & Two
Lord Edward	Day One

For Lunch

O'Neills	Days One & Two
The Brazen Head	Day Sixteen & Eighteen
O'Donoghue's (15 Suffolk Street)	Day Eleven
The Oval	Day Three

For Dinner

Darwins	Days Two & Fourteen

Sights

Glasnevin Cemetery	Day Twelve
Kilmainham Gaol (prison)	Day Eleven
St. Stephen's Green	Day Four
Easter Rising walking tours	Days Three & Thirty
Phoenix Park	Day Two
Food, Folklore, and Fairies	Days Twenty-Five Twenty-six

Howth

Pubs

Waterside Pub	Day Twenty-Nine
The Abbey	Day Twenty-Nine
The Bloody Stream	Day Twenty-Nine

For Lunch

Waterside Pub	Day Twenty-Nine
The Abbey	Day Twenty-Nine

Limerick

Hotel

Jurys	Day Seven

Pubs

Flannery's	Day Seven
Old Quarter	Day Seven

For Lunch

The Locke	Day Seven

For Dinner

Texas Steakhouse	Day Nine

Sights

King John's Castle	Day Seven
Bunratty Castle and Folk Park	Day Eight
Village of Adare	Day Nine

Wicklow

Pubs

Johnnie Fox's	Day Thirty

For Dinner

Johnnie Fox's	Day Thirty

Sights

Glendalough monastic ruins	Day Twenty-Five

HELPFUL WEB ADDRESSES

Darwins: www.darwins.ie/
Mary O'Grady: www.irishtravelplans.net/
    maryogrady@eircom.net
Office of Tourism: www.visitdublin.com/
Jurys Inn Christchurch: www.jurysinns.com/christchurch/
Black Taxi Tours: www.blacktaxitours.com/
Kilmainham Gaol: www.visitdublin.com/
Glasnevin Cemetery: www.glasnevintrust.ie/
Irish Rail: www.irishrail.ie/
Irish Bus: www.buseireann.ie/
Dingle Bay Hotel: www.dinglebayhotel.com/
Fungie the Dolphin: www.dingledolphin.com/
Guinness Storehouse: www.guinness-storehouse.com/
1916 Rebellion Walking Tour: www.1916rising.com/
Rebel Walking Tour: www.sinnfeinbookshop.com/

I leave you with one of my favorite Irish blessings:

May the road rise up to meet you.
May the wind always be at your back.
May the sun shine warm upon your face,
and rains fall soft on your fields.
And until we meet again,
May God hold you in the palm of His hand.

NOTES

NOTES

NOTES

NOTES

NOTES

NOTES

NOTES

NOTES

NOTES

NOTES

NOTES

NOTES

Made in United States
Orlando, FL
20 April 2022

17030306R00077